A Gift from Saint Francis

A Gift from Saint Francis
The First Crèche

Written by Joanna Cole

Illustrated by Michèle Lemieux

Morrow Junior Books \ New York

Library of Congress Cataloging-in-Publication Data
Cole, Joanna.
A gift from Saint Francis : the first crèche / by Joanna Cole ;
illustrations by Michèle Lemieux.
p. cm.
Summary: Traces the life of the Italian who turned his back on his
family's wealth to help the poor and teach about God. Discusses
Francis' role in the making of the first crèche.
ISBN 0-688-06502-3. ISBN 0-688-06503-1 (lib. bdg.)
1. Francis, of Assisi, Saint, 1182-1226—Contributions in
development of crèches (Nativity scenes)—Juvenile literature.
2. Crèches (Nativity scenes)—History—Juvenile literature.
[1. Francis, of Assisi, Saint, 1182-1226. 2. Saints. 3. Crèches
(Nativity scenes)—History.] I. Lemieux, Michèle, ill. II. Title.
BX4700.F69C65 1989
246'.55—dc19
[B]
[92]   88-22048   CIP   AC

To my parents, Betty and Mario
J.C.

To my parents, Suzanne and Lionel
M.L.

For I would make a memorial of that Child who was born in Bethlehem, and in some sort behold with bodily eyes His infant hardships; how He lay in a manger on hay, with the ox and ass standing by.

—The words of Saint Francis quoted in
The First Life of Saint Francis of Assisi
by Brother Thomas of Celano
A.D. 1229

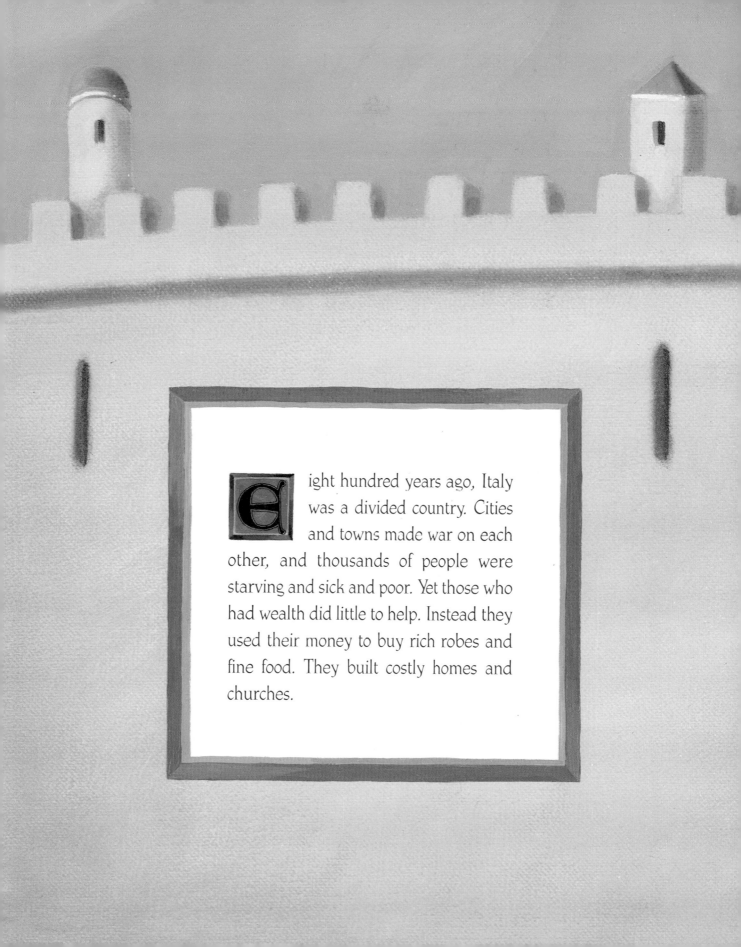

eight hundred years ago, Italy was a divided country. Cities and towns made war on each other, and thousands of people were starving and sick and poor. Yet those who had wealth did little to help. Instead they used their money to buy rich robes and fine food. They built costly homes and churches.

 n the midst of all this greed and suffer-
ing, a rich man's son was born in the hill
town of Assisi. To make him happy, his
parents gave him whatever he wanted. But they
could not spoil Francis. His loving nature drew
people to him. Every day he played in the cobbled
streets, laughing and singing with his friends.

As he grew to manhood, Francis thought more
and more about God, and he felt a desire to help
the poor. Often he left his father's house with a
purse full of money and gave it to the first poor per-
son he met. Once when he had no money, he took
the cloak from his own shoulders and gave it to a
beggar.

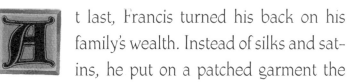 t last, Francis turned his back on his family's wealth. Instead of silks and satins, he put on a patched garment the color of dust and earth. He owned no shoes, carried no money, and begged for his food. Francis wanted to show that happiness came not from money, but from loving God and feeling loved by Him.

When his friends and neighbors saw Francis in his beggar's clothes, they called him *"Pazzo, pazzo,"* which means "Crazy man, crazy man." His father declared that Francis was no longer his son.

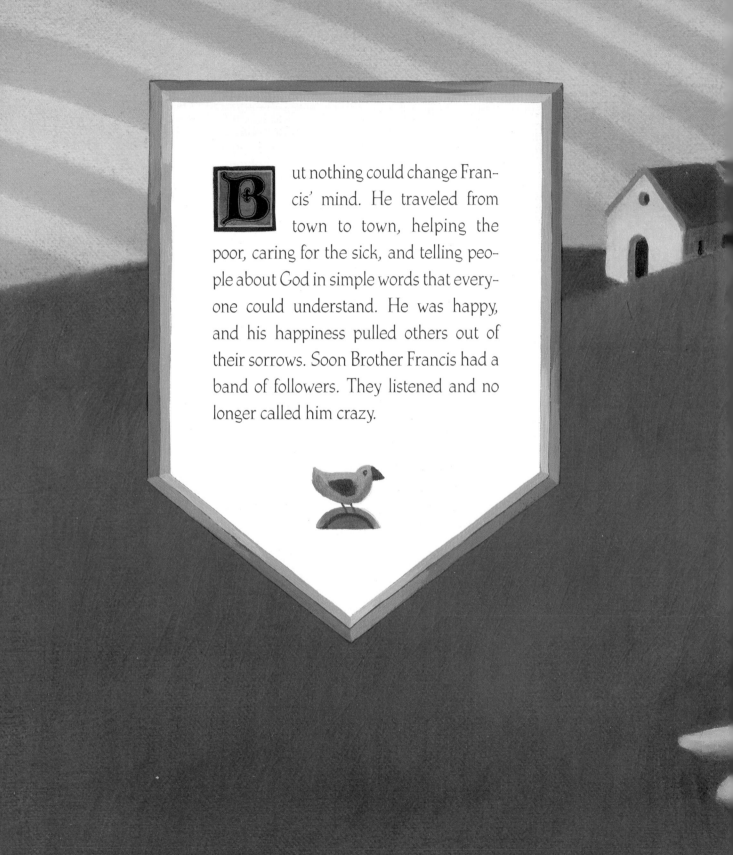

But nothing could change Francis' mind. He traveled from town to town, helping the poor, caring for the sick, and telling people about God in simple words that everyone could understand. He was happy, and his happiness pulled others out of their sorrows. Soon Brother Francis had a band of followers. They listened and no longer called him crazy.

he love in Francis flowed to all God's creatures. If he saw a worm in the road, he moved it carefully to one side so it would not be stepped on. He freed rabbits from the snare and rescued lambs from the market. He even preached to the birds, which perched on his arms and shoulders without fear.

In those days, people did not celebrate Christmas as we do now. They had never seen a Christmas tree, had never sung a Christmas carol, and they probably did not give or receive presents.

But Francis believed that Jesus' birthday should be made special. He wanted everyone to sing songs at Christmas and to give extra food to their animals. He asked people to scatter grain along the roads so the birds he loved so much could join the Christmas feast.

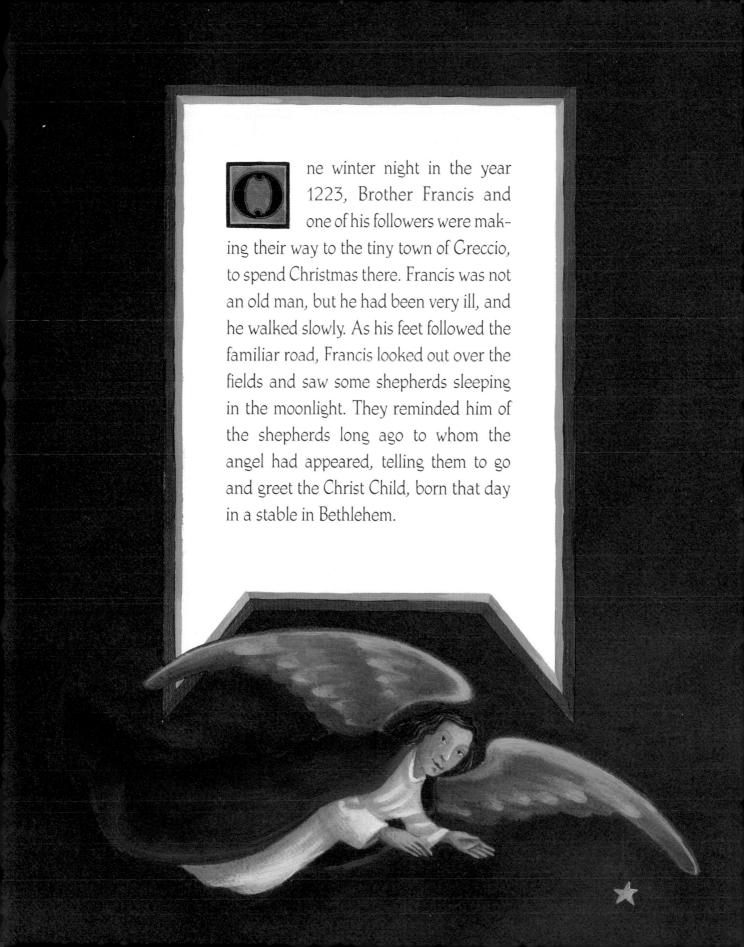

One winter night in the year 1223, Brother Francis and one of his followers were making their way to the tiny town of Greccio, to spend Christmas there. Francis was not an old man, but he had been very ill, and he walked slowly. As his feet followed the familiar road, Francis looked out over the fields and saw some shepherds sleeping in the moonlight. They reminded him of the shepherds long ago to whom the angel had appeared, telling them to go and greet the Christ Child, born that day in a stable in Bethlehem.

rancis had seen the shepherds, and now he longed to see the rest of the Christmas story with his own eyes. More than that, he wanted to share it with others.

So Francis planned a surprise for the people of the town. He needed a wooden feeding trough, a load of hay, a few animals, and some people to dress in costumes. As always, there were many who wanted to help Brother Francis.

y Christmas Eve, word had spread that something wonderful was going to happen on a wooded hill outside the town, and people came from all around. The light from their torches flickered through the trees as they climbed the hillside paths. Their excited voices echoed through the woods.

When they arrived at the spot Francis had chosen, a shout of joy went up from the crowd. Never had the poor farmers of Greccio imagined that they would look upon the holy scene they had heard about since childhood. There was the infant Jesus, lying in a manger, with Mary and Joseph watching over him, and a donkey and an ox standing near.

In the voice they knew so well, Francis read to the people from the Bible. He told how Jesus was born in a stable and laid in a manger because there was no room at the inn.

Lovingly, Francis lifted the baby in his arms. He urged the people to put aside their quarrels and treat each other with kindness, as Jesus wanted them to.

Then he called the children forward and asked them to sing to the Christ Child. Their lullaby to Jesus may have been the world's first Christmas carol.

ot long after that Christmas Eve on the hillside, Brother Francis died. But the people never forgot the beautiful nativity scene he had made for them. Year after year, they recreated it in the same place.

Soon other towns took up the custom as well. In time, Brother Francis' idea spread all over the world. Now, wherever you go at Christmastime, you may see the figures of Mary, Joseph, and the others watching over baby Jesus in the stable.

This was Saint Francis' gift to us—the crèche, a symbol of hope, peace, and joy.

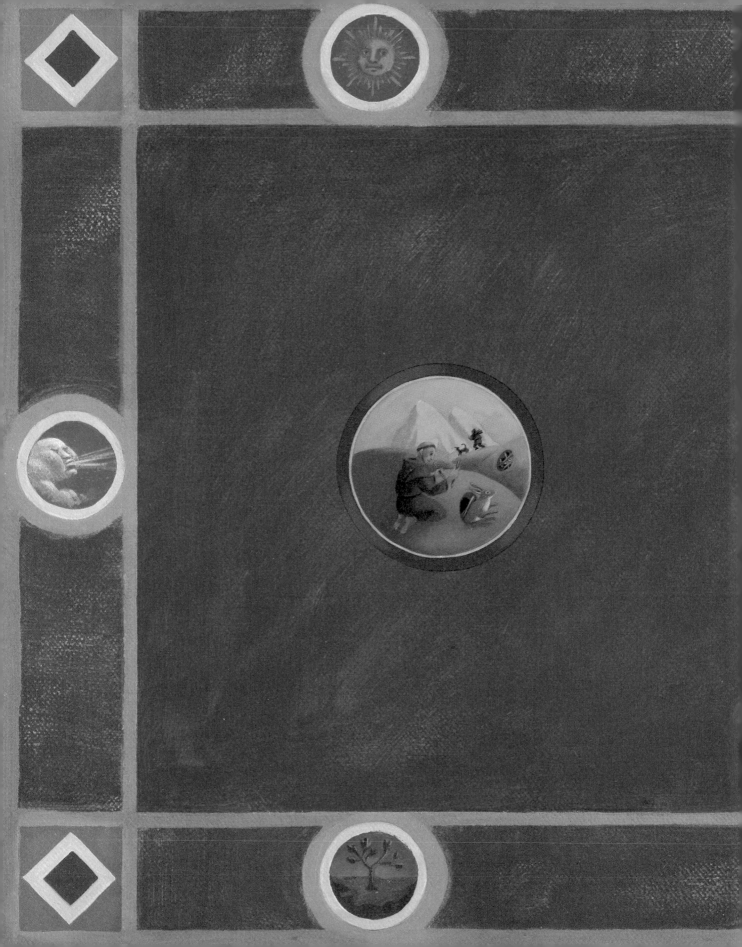